PRACTICE GROWTH SUPERPOWERS: How To Get Better Clients And Generate More Profits

ISBN: 978-1-5272-6536-3

Disclaimer

The material in this publication is of the nature of general comment only, and does not represent professional advice. It is not intended to provide specific guidance for particular circumstances and it should not be relied on as the basis for any decision to take action or not take action on any matter which it covers.

Readers should obtain professional advice where appropriate, before making any such decision.

To the maximum extent permitted by law, the author and publisher disclaim all responsibility and liability to any person, arising directly or indirectly from any person taking or not taking action based on the information in this publication.

PRACTICE GROWTH SUPERPOWERS

How To Get Better Clients And Generate More Profits

Amanda C. Watts

Contents

WHO IS THIS BOOK FOR?

This book is for trailblazers, shot takers, impact seekers and visionary accountants, outsourced CFOs and financial coaches of all kinds. It is for those among you who are willing to break the mould and wonder why no one else wants to.

You challenge the traditional way of thinking, you embrace a new way of running your practice and you are focused on gaining back your time whilst making the biggest contribution.

You don't accept your destiny, you define it. You don't accept the status-quo, you drive the profession forward; despite the odds.

Whilst the rest of the profession strive for average and cling desperately to the status quo, you are in the minority. You are one of the few who are willing to shake things up, try new methods and models, and have way more fun in the process.

You are VITAL to the success of your client's businesses.... And you always will be.

WHAT I DID AND HOW YOU CAN DO IT TOO

Chances are we have never met. If reading this book is your first experience of me then I must share something with you. I am not an accountant.

I have not spent years learning how to do accounting or CFO work, and I have never ever claimed to be an expert in 'accounting'.

But don't stop reading.

Right now you are wanting some help with the exact thing I can help you with - Marketing high value advisory/consulting services and getting great paying clients that don't question you on price.

You see, just like you, I too offer advisory/consulting services.

I own a highly successful advisory business, working an average of 5 hours a day 4 days a week at most. Our turnover is 7 figures and our net profit ranges from 56% - 80% depending on our marketing activity.

My offer is slightly different to one that you might offer at his moment in time, but that is where the differences end.

Let me share my story with you quickly.

For many years I ran what we would call a 'done for you' agency. In this agency we would carry out the marketing work for you... post your social media, write your copy, design your website. But I was working 16 hour days and had a huge team to manage. Profits were tight. I was stressed. I didn't see my children enough and I certainly didn't get paid my worth.

This scenario is not unlike your current situation. You run a 'done for you' accounting practice. You gather the information (which in itself can be pushing water up a hill) and then do all the compliance work on behalf of your client. You submit tax returns, do the year end for them and generally run around looking after your clients, chasing them, nagging them and feeling frustrated by them, whilst they get on with their day jobs and growing their business. Often your profits are tight and you are stressed. Worse still your clients don't value the work you carry out for them, they question you on price and try to bargain with you for a discount.

Now back to me for a second. I didn't want to carry on in my 'done-for-you' situation. So I decided it was time to change the way I ran my business.

I knew a ton about marketing so I started to do more advisory/consulting work. I would help my clients by advising them around marketing and sales, as well as doing some of the work for them.

I started to keep them accountable for the actions they said they would do. I became a cheerleader for them, building their confidence.

Most importantly, they started to see real results from our work together.

As time went on I learnt so much from my clients that I also started advising around pricing their services, and what their service offering should be, I helped them with time management and systemising their practice.

My services were less 'done-for-you' and more 'done-with-you'.

My turnover went up. My profits increased exponentially. My take home pay went up. My working hours decreased.

Most importantly, my client's results catapulted through the roof.

I was no longer stressed. I saw way more of my darling children. And joy came back into my world.

The words to describe my business are often called consulting or advisory. You may also see it as teaching, mentoring or coaching.

But in all honesty don't focus on what it is called. Focus on the *transformation* of my client's businesses and their lives. That was the biggest shift for them, and me.

Now back to you again.

Your future could be like my current reality, and all it takes is a shift in mindset and a tweak to your 'offer'.

Your accounting or outsourced CFO practice may currently be a 'done-for-you' practice where most of your work gives you very low profits. But we can change this. You can introduce a service where a larger percentage of your work gives you huge profits. You can be an advisor, consultant, coach, mentor or trainer. You can get better clients. You can have more profits.

I am not saying stop being an accountant or outsourced CFO. I have never stopped being a marketer. What I am saying is take your expertise that you have spent years studying and taking exams in, and start to share your knowledge to help grow your clients businesses.

It;s time to step up and give your clients more support, keep them truly accountable, help them achieve their business and life goals and become that VITAL asset to your clients, to the point where they pay you handsomely for your services, because you are changing their lives. Be so VITAL that they couldn't run their business without you.

In this book I am going to share with you the methodology I have used to help thousands of accountants, outsourced CFOs and financial coaches over the years. I am going to share how they have introduced leveraged advisory/consulting and have clients pay them their worth.

PART ONE - WHY THERE IS A TON OF MONEY IN ADVISORY/CONSULTING

The only way I can describe advisory is like this:

VITAL: absolutely necessary; essential.

And there are a few reasons (aside from my personal experience) that make me say this.

According to Forbes, accounting and bookkeeping is the number one most profitable industry right now.

And here's why this is important...

You probably hear every day that you should offer some sort of advisory services. According to research from Bill.com and CPA.com, 58.9% of buyers are purchasing advisory/consulting services of some kind from their accountant and 25% of accountants are offering themselves as outsourced CFOs.

Bundling and packaging up value-rich services are on the rise. And advisory/consulting, outsourced CFO work, and cash flow analysis are all very well suited to non-hourly billing models.

Another very important point that has to be noted is that industry expertise is in demand.

Whilst in the past, accounting practices offered the same services, in the same way, to all businesses... today's savvy buyers have cottoned on to the power of working with an expert and/or specialist. This has seen a surge of accounting practices become increasingly specialised, attracting clients in specific and niche industries.

When buyers were asked what they would change about the accounting practices they worked with, 27% said they wanted them to have more familiarity with their business and industry. That's a huge percentage of buyers wanting an expert/specialist.

So whilst other accountants are still pushing traditional compliance services to potential buyers, you have a huge advantage if you decide to offer advisory/consulting services to niche markets.

Advisory/consulting services have something that most other accounting services don't have.

Very High Net Profits

A great thing about advisory/consulting is it's very high in terms of net profits.

To deliver advisory/consulting services you need very little in the way of tools. You do not need fancy equipment, office space or fancy apps/software.

Marketing costs can be minimal (as you need fewer clients because they are higher revenue) and often just a laptop and your mobile are all you need.

What many accountants, outsourced CFOs and financial coaches need to understand is that if they don't offer advisory services then not only will other practices scoop up the highly profitable work, but so will other competitors outside of their industry.

Namely business coaches.

According to leading coaching company Lequin, coaches charge between £500 and £1250 for a two hour session. The difference in their prices come down to confidence, experience and often the marketing and sales systems that have been put in place. Sometimes it comes down to quality of service.

I also know for a fact that some coaches charge way more than this and class themselves as trainers/consultants. These trainers/consultants can charge upwards of £5000 per month to work with them. I know this to be fact as this is what I charge now for 1:1 support, and so do many of my peers with my experience and knowledge.

To be fair, traditional business coaches can have a grasp of simple finances. They can understand profit and loss, and can advise on how to increase the top line of a business. However they rarely have formal qualifications when it comes to coaching/the numbers/finances and often set up their business through leveraging a franchise or 'giving it a go'. These self taught coaches lack a deeper level of understanding of what it really takes to run a profitable business that can scale effectively or be sold. An accountant/outsourced CFO can spot trends in financial performance faster and with way more expertise than a business coach. This unique speed and expertise will change the fortunes of the business.

Now you have seen what business coaches can charge, without specific expertise in understanding the numbers, why can you not do this too, knowing *you bring more to the table than most business coaches do?*

Reasons You Should Offer Advisory/Consulting Services:

The fact of the matter is, if you have any experience in running a practice and interpreting the numbers then you really need to add advisory services to your accounting practice. Not only so you can make more profit but so you can make a bigger impact on/transform your client's businesses too.

Advisory/consulting is way more profitable than compliance alone.

Let me share with you why this is true.

Reason 1 - Monthly Recurring Revenue

A lot of accountants/outsourced CFOs think that advisory/consulting should be priced on an hourly basis, but this thinking will lead to burnout.

After I got burnout back in 2017, I knew I had to change the way I priced my services. So I found another way to price. Right now I am going to share how to avoid pricing by the hour and what to do instead.

I want to show you how your practice needs to price on MRR - **Monthly Recurring Revenue.**

Yes, you want your clients to pay monthly.

It's good for the client. And it's great for your cash flow and peace of mind.

MRR gives you certainty that you'll get the money in the bank every month, you don't have to constantly sell and get new clients every week and you don't live in feast or famine.

Debtor days go down. Paydays go up.

If that scenario sounds appealing, then I am going to show you how to achieve this, right here in these pages of this book.

And remember, this can be part time, with a small (tiny) team and from home.

For most accountants, that's a big reason to offer advisory.

The predictability, and not stressing about money.

The model is: fewer clients, higher revenue.

Reason 2 - Higher Revenue

When offering advisory services you don't have to worry about selling to thousands of businesses in the hope they may pay you 1-2k a year for your compliance services.

You don't have to be compared on price with other accountants.

You don't have to have a huge team to do the work for your hundreds of clients.

You don't have squeezed margins with huge outgoings. You don't have to have a thousand clients to make a million (if a million is what you want).

Because you don't have to get hundreds of clients, you have more time on your hands, and you can then serve your advisory clients so well and charge your worth/the value you provide.

This means the majority of your revenue should be net profit, and end up in your pocket, rather than paying for a team/software.

That money is for you to spend on your family, holidays/vacations, houses, giving to charity or your vinyl collection should you so wish.

The money is yours (and the tax man's - but we all know higher tax often equals higher revenue).

Reason 3 - Happy Clients With A Strong ROI

Like I said, advisory means you are serving your clients better, offering a transformation to their business and life rather than just a transactional service (like compliance). You are actually getting them results in their business that you can't get them when only offering compliance.

You are helping your clients be more lucrative, they have a Return On Their Investment with you instead of just being a cost to them. Your services and you become VITAL.

Reason 4 - Advisory/Consulting Is Easier To Sell

Contrary to what you might currently believe, advisory is easier to sell than compliance.

The reason why is because of the VALUE Ladder.

You see, whenever someone buys from you, they are getting value. However this value increases/decreases depending on what they buy and what they receive.

The Value Ladder

There are 3 different kinds of service models in the accounting/consulting world. Each service model offers different value to those you work with.

One model is more prominent than others right now. And unfortunately it's the one that brings the least value to your clients, and delivers the practice owner the least profits.

Let's explore all three now.

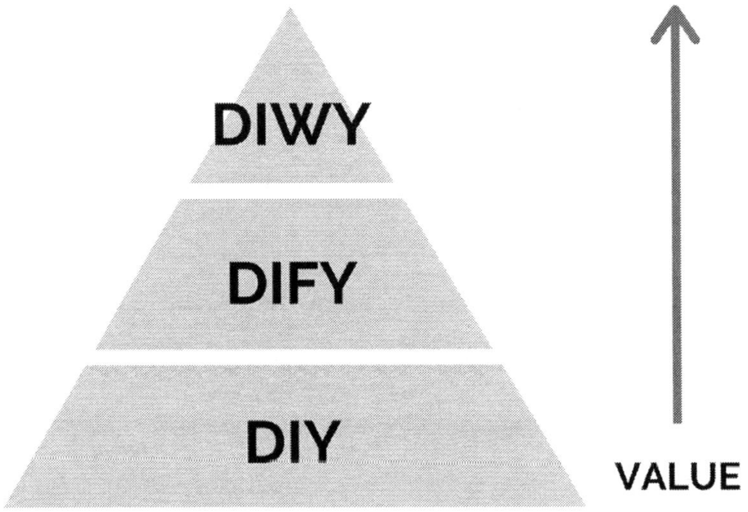

Model One: The 'Do-It-Yourself' Model

Let's start with the model that most new business owners opt for. 'Do-It-Yourself' accounting/admin/back office work.

This approach is often taken by new businesses or uneducated businesses.

These businesses often believe that buying their own software (e.g. Xero or Quickbooks) will give them everything they need to know about doing their books.

Which, as you were once a start-up, you know this thinking is incorrect. There is more to doing your books than just using software.

These new or uneducated business owners haven't yet seen the value in getting help with their finances, and often question you on price if they do approach you.

Model Two: The 'Do-It-For-You' Model

So let's talk about this business model and the mindset of the business owner looking for this model.

The 'do-it-for-you' model is where a business owner wants their pain taken away. They are often driven to choose services that save them time, and take away the task of having to learn/understand anything to do with the numbers.

The 'do-it-for-you' model will appeal to the business owner who see accounting as a necessity to be compliant, but have yet to see the value of anything more than ticking off the boxes and completing the right forms, at the right time in the right way.

Some business owners will pay well for these services, but as an accountant it can be hard to differentiate your offering when just 'doing-it-for-them'. Finding the clients that will pay you well for these services can also be an onerous task in itself.

Model Three: The 'Do-It-With-You' Model

Now let's talk about the top of the value ladder. Where you have an unparalleled service, offer and value proposition.

The 'do-it-with-you' model is focused on transforming the results of a business and the business owner's lives. The 'do-it-with-you' model is about understanding the goals and aspirations of the business owner and working with them over a number of years to help them achieve said goals.

It's a mixture of ticking the compliance boxes coupled with educating the client on what actions they need to take, advising on opportunities and maximising positive outcomes that align with their goals. It's accountability, insight, planning and advisory/consulting all rolled into one.

In a business owner's world this is the pinnacle of desirability because you are helping them understand and get results faster, whilst doing some of the heavy lifting for them. This service offering transforms lives.

Which is why advisory/consulting is the easiest thing to sell. But in fact so few of you offer it because you are focused on just getting that next client, filling your practice with paying customers (even if they pay badly) and often onboarding compliance only clients. Thus providing a transaction instead of a transformation.

Let's recap the benefits of offering advisory/consulting services to your clients:

1. Advisory/consulting is much **easier to sell** because it sits at the top of the value ladder.

2. Advisory/consulting is **very profitable** as it needs just you, your knowledge and a tiny team to support you. No premises or fancy software is required.

3. It gives you **monthly recurring revenue**, peace of mind and excellent cash flow.

4. It **makes you VITAL** to a business, so when the economic climate has a downturn you are not seen as a cost but as an investment.

All of these reasons represent why advisory/consulting is a huge opportunity for you right now, and how you can make great money whilst impacting people's lives.

What Advisory/Consulting Really Is

Let's talk about what advisory/consulting really is - because there are a lot of misconceptions about it.

The first thing, according to the dictionary advisory is:

Advisory: *having or consisting in the power to make recommendations but not to take action enforcing them.*

An advisor is: a person who gives advice in a particular field.

Consulting: *the business of giving expert advice to other professionals.*

A consultant is: a person who provides expert advice professionally.

That's it.

The reason why so many accountants fail to offer advisory/consulting is because of the myths surrounding it.

Myth 1: You need expensive technology. Whilst software can be a supportive tool, advisory/consulting isn't about using software. Being an advisor/consultant is about asking questions and analysing the numbers in front of you, and matching up results to the goals of the business owner.

Myth 2: You don't have the skills/experience. If you are a qualified accountant/CFO, and have previously worked in industry or another accounting practice you will have developed many skills and have much experience. Even the act of setting up and running your own business increases your level of knowledge exponentially. Start believing in your own value, and you can start to make a bigger impact.

Myth 3: You need to be an extrovert to be an advisor. Often it is the quiet leader that helps a business more than the extrovert dictator. Your unemotional listening skills make you the smartest person in the room. Your insights are what business owners need, not someone who shouts loudly.

The 3% Rule

One thing I have noticed when I speak to 'experts' is that many know as little as 3% more than the person they are advising/consulting with.

Which opens up a whole new world of opportunity for the accountant that has studied accounting, passed exams and has worked with businesses before. A qualified accountant understands numbers and can translate what they mean. This knowledge helps clients hit their goals.

Please note that I am not condoning winging it and pretending you have the knowledge. I am saying get started, and offer advice to business owners that don't know what you know. 3% is a huge knowledge gap.

The secret to advisory is to know more than your client does. You don't need to know more than the rest of the world, they are not paying you, you just need to know a little more than the person you are advising.

The bottom line is that you can be an advisor/consultant. Everything you have learnt and done to the present day has set you up to be one.

If you can get your client results faster than they would on their own, that is all you need.

When someone is looking to buy from you they want to feel confident in the results you can get them and the value you provide. If you can demonstrate said results and value, you will get advisory clients that won't question you on price.

My journey is a case in point. When I first started teaching small businesses how to use social media, I had limited knowledge myself. I knew 3% more than my clients. I had a few months experience of Twitter and Facebook, but had managed to use the platforms to get clients and I taught my experience. I didn't use the lack of knowledge as an excuse, I just used it as a fuel to learn more, fast.

So the fact is, if you are freaked out about offering advisory services and your lack of credentials I totally understand. But you have what it takes and some.

How Much Do You Want It?

Later in this book I am going to talk about getting leads, clients and scaling your practice.

But before we go any further let's get real.

Creating A Freedom Practice vs A Monster Business

Many accountants wake up one day and decide they want to branch out on their own. They're ready to take control of their own destiny, they want more freedom and control over their own lives and start working for themselves.

They start out feeling excited and passionate, but soon end up overworked, underpaid and severely stressed out. In fact, they were often far better off when they were working for somebody else.

I call this situation having a JOB: Which stands for Just Over Broke.

These 'jobbies' have been sold the dream of starting, growing and exiting a business. They think that they're building something of value so that they can eventually sell up for a lottery-win figure and retire to the Bahamas or spend their days playing golf.

However in all reality, the saleable value of an accounting business upon sale has dramatically decreased over recent years. The traditional accounting firm competes on price during trading times and gets offered a minimal exit value upon sale. This means jobbies are putting in all that effort for little to no return on their hard work.

To make matters worse, the firms that jobbies build are full of Vampire clients. Vampire clients ask for their pound of flesh, and in return leave the business owner and their team bleeding at the neck - both financially and emotionally.

Accountants are sold a dream: the idea of a 7 figure business that gives them lots of money and time in their lives. Yet in reality, they simply end up with squeezed profits, heartburn and misery.

There is something else to bear in mind, too. Traditional accounting businesses are commoditised. They are seen as a cost to their clients rather than an investment and subsequently are not valued. To make money the firm owner and their team create a monster of a business that neither the owners nor staff enjoy working in.

A Monster Business looks something like this:

- One million turnover
- 1000 clients paying £1000 a year for compliance work (if advisory is given the advice is often given for free)
- 20-40 staff needed to service the clients due to the high volume of compliance work
- Low profit margins
- High overheads
- Not agile
- Less responsive
- Lots of systems and software required

But there is another way.

A FREEDOM PRACTICE

We tend to think that there are only two ways to earn money: getting a job or starting a business.

There is, however, a third option: creating a practice.

Only a certain kind of person can create a practice. And this certain kind of person has to have the right practice model for profits and scalability.

A Freedom Practice can be created by any accountant, outsourced CFO and financial advisor/consultant that position themselves as VITAL.

Trust me on this. Creating a practice means that your dreams are tangible after all, and these dreams can be fulfilled in as little as 3 years.

A practice is built by a certain kind of person from certain professions including: dentists, surgeons, business coaches. Crucially, accountants, financial advisors and outsourced CFOs are all capable of building a practice too.

Unlike a business, a practice is based on one thing: the expertise of the practice owner.

A practice relies on the owner bringing their knowledge and selling their expertise. Everyone else in the practice is there to do one thing: support the expert.

Support can come from admin, marketing and sales, any compliance team that might be in place, contractors and offshore/outsourcing companies. The ultimate goal is to free up the practice owners time to enable them to bring in money and make an impact.

Unlike a traditional Monster Business, the structure of a Freedom Practice is quite simple, a few key team members and medium/high revenue clients create very high profits.

The key team roles in a practice are::

- The Expert
- An Integrator
- Marketing & Sales Support
- Small Accounting Support Team (Compliance work, etc.)
- Operations Support

A practice can turn over 1 million per year with a lean team of 4-6 people, including the expert practice owner.

In this context, the expert is typically the advisor, consultant or financial strategist.

Practices are liberating when built well. They have very low start up costs, can re-invest as cash flow is generated and profits are good.

Costly considerations such as websites, vision and mission statements, raising capital and investing in software can all be held off until much further down the line - if at all.

A good practice will operate with low running costs and high margins.

A practice can rarely be sold upon exit, so you need to be making good money along the way. This will then allow you to invest in wealth building with your high take home pay and huge profits from the practice. You reap your income today, rather than wait for the sale of your business when you retire.

The practice expert is the go-to for all the thinking, strategising and product or service creation. They're irreplaceable. They have to show up and deliver, and they have to work hard at the beginning of their practice journey.

I am not making a case for one or the other. I know of a few accounting firm owners who have a hybrid of 'business and practice' and have thrived with both offerings.

Personally, I have worked in many businesses. It was enough for me to realise I never wanted to own one.

Instead, I wanted to run a practice and, after a few years of initial hard graft, I now have a Freedom Practice.

Every week, I spend a few hours with clients and a further few on marketing. I have a leveraged delivery model that generates very high revenue and strong profits.

A Freedom Practice looks like this...

- One million turnover
- 100 clients paying £6000-£10000 a year for advisory/consulting services
- 2-4 staff needed to service the clients and do marketing
- High-profit margins
- Low overheads

- Very agile
- Highly responsive
- Streamlined systems and minimum software required

FREEDOM PRACTICE	MONSTER BUSINESS
Small Team	Large Team
Based Around Owner	Based On Systems
High Profit Margins	Low Profit Margins
Low Overheads	High Overheads
Highly Agile	Slow And Cumbersome
Simple Systems	Complex Systems
Simple App Stack	Complex App Stack
Niche	Generalist

Time For Some Honesty

You will have heard many times that accountants should take their name off the door. Conventional wisdom dictates that they should build a business around their business name, and their team rather than themselves, so that the business can be sold with ease when they retire.

This is terrible advice for a practice owner, who wants to be professionally famous, and financially free now. A practice is built around the owner, namely their personal brand, knowledge and expertise. Therefore, when creating a website something like www.yourname.com will fit the bill nicely. You can check out mine at www.amandacwatts.com.

I come across many people running accountancy and outsourced CFO firms receiving well-meaning but often bad advice. This is because it comes from people who think they know how to build a business, not a practice.

Indeed, I see accountants being shown how to build Monster Businesses and being told to embrace the 'McDonalds' cookie-cutter way of doing things.

This means:

- Falling into the trap of more and more low value clients
- Spending too much money on software packages to help them deliver compliance
- Thinking systemising their practice is the only way to maximise profits

There is much proof in the world that there are many successful people who have built both a business and a practice alongside each other.

Richard Branson is one example. He has his personal brand where he gets paid to speak, earns book royalties and runs retreats for entrepreneurs; this is his practice. He also runs the Virgin Group as a business. His practice will undoubtedly deliver him more profits and take home pay now than his businesses do.

If Richard re-invests some of this take-home pay into wealth building (which he undoubtedly does) he will have income from this money when he retires. He does not put all his eggs into one basket and hope that his businesses will be worth something when it comes to selling/exiting.

Let me also tell you about Ben (name changed for confidentiality reasons). Ben runs both a business and a practice simultaneously.

His accounting business turns over around $3million dollars and employs over 40 staff.

Let's be conservative and say this is around 76,800 hours of delivery time . This equates to an average of $39 an hour earnings for the work done.

Meanwhile, his advisory/consulting practice turns over just shy of $1million dollars and is just himself and a very small admin support team.

His practice currently has 32 clients and takes him and his team less than a week per month for delivery. That's 480 hours a year for a million dollar practice. Making $2,083 an hour earnings for the work done.

You don't need me to tell you which one of these set-ups is more profitable and gives you time and financial freedom.

When talking to Ben about his business and practice I asked him whether he'd build his business and practice in the same way if he had the chance to start over.

His answer came as no surprise: he would set up a practice and not a business if he could have a 'do-over'.

Now that you have a clearer understanding of the difference between a business and a practice, let's crunch some numbers.

What revenue do you want to make through your advisory/consulting practice, and how many clients do you really need to reach this revenue?

Once we know these figures we can then work out how long it will take for you to reach your revenue target.

Let's look at the amount of monthly recurring revenue you want to add to your practice over the next 12 months.

Example:

Desired MRR: 20k extra a month

Now let's look at your service offering. How much will it cost to work with you each year (this can be made up of a compliance offering and/or advisory)

Example:

Compliance/Advisory offer: 6k per year

Let's turn this figure into monthly payments 6000/12 = 500 MRR

If you are looking to add 20k a month to your MRR then you would need to get 40 clients in the next year.

This is equal to just over 3 clients a month. At the end of 12 months your MRR would be 20k a month.

Now, as you know, accountants tend to keep their clients for a lot longer than 12 months, averaging 7 years or more. This means that it would take less than 3 years of taking on 3 clients a month to smash a 500k revenue goal. And less than 5 years to smash 7 figures and a MRR of 90k.

If you increased your advisory service offering to 10k a year, your MRR per client would be 833 a month.

If you wanted a firm that had a million pound run rate, you would only need 100 clients to achieve this.

8 new clients a month over 12 months.

Maybe more realistically 4 new clients a month over 24 months.

Or even 2 a month over 36 months.

Now if this seems like pie in the sky please note I have worked with firms with a turnover of 200k and have increased to 1m in as little as 16 months.

I have clients that regularly get paid 1-2k a month for advisory/consulting services.

And it's my mission to ensure you get paid at least 500 a month (6k a year) for compliance and very basic advisory.

It can be done. I have seen it done hundreds of times. Check out the MRR plan that we use in our Momentum programme to work out desired MRR.

It clearly shows how onboarding just 3 clients a month will enable you to create a Freedom Practice.

YOUR MRR PLAN

YEAR 1	MONTH 1	MONTH 2	MONTH 3	MONTH 4	MONTH 5	MONTH 6	MONTH 7	MONTH 8	MONTH 9	MONTH 10	MONTH 11	MONTH 12	
NUMBER OF CLIENTS	3	6	9	12	15	18	21	24	27	30	33	36	TOTAL
MONTHLY FEE													
250	750	1500	2250	3000	3750	4500	5250	6000	6750	7500	8250	9000	**58500**
500	1500	3000	4500	6000	7500	9000	10500	12000	13500	15000	16500	18000	**117000**
1000	3000	6000	9000	12000	15000	18000	21000	24000	27000	30000	33000	36000	**234000**
2000	6000	12000	18000	24000	30000	36000	42000	48000	54000	60000	66000	72000	**468000**

YEAR 2	MONTH 1	MONTH 2	MONTH 3	MONTH 4	MONTH 5	MONTH 6	MONTH 7	MONTH 8	MONTH 9	MONTH 10	MONTH 11	MONTH 12	
NUMBER OF CLIENTS	39	42	45	48	51	54	57	60	63	66	69	72	TOTAL
MONTHLY FEE													
250	9750	10500	11250	12000	12750	13500	14250	15000	15750	16500	17250	18000	**166500**
500	19500	21000	22500	24000	25500	27000	28500	30000	31500	33000	34500	36000	**333000**
1000	39000	42000	45000	48000	51000	54000	57000	60000	63000	66000	69000	72000	**666000**
2000	78000	84000	90000	96000	102000	108000	114000	120000	126000	132000	138000	144000	**1332000**

YEAR 3	MONTH 1	MONTH 2	MONTH 3	MONTH 4	MONTH 5	MONTH 6	MONTH 7	MONTH 8	MONTH 9	MONTH 10	MONTH 11	MONTH 12	
NUMBER OF CLIENTS	75	78	81	84	87	90	93	96	99	102	105	108	TOTAL
MONTHLY FEE													
250	18750	19500	20250	21000	21750	22500	23250	24000	24750	25500	26350	27000	**274500**
500	37500	39000	40500	42000	435000	45000	46500	48000	49500	51000	525000	54000	**549000**
1000	75000	78000	81000	84000	87000	90000	93000	96000	99000	102000	105000	108000	**1098000**
2000	15000	156000	162000	168000	174000	180000	186000	192000	198000	204000	210000	216000	**2196000**

PART TWO - HOW TO IDENTIFY THE RIGHT CLIENTS

The first thing you need to do before trying to find clients is identify what kind of business is going to be a good business for you to offer advisory services to.

For example, say you want to target start-up businesses. On the surface this might seem like a good kind of business to target. Right now, here in the UK, there are 2500 businesses starting every day.

But in reality only 80% of businesses make it to the second year of business and by year 5 only 56% are left trading. Considering you want to keep a client for 7 years or more this cuts your chances of reliable monthly recurring revenue significantly.

If start up businesses are not a good fit for advisory/consulting then what/who does make an ideal client/business to work with?

Well, quite simply an ideal client is one that gets the fastest results working with you, has a strong turnover, and can be found and is active online.

It is easier to get a 500 a month MRR client, or even a 2000 a month MRR client if that client has a turnover of 500k or above.

It is also easier to make a quick impact/get quick results if the business is established and has a product or service that they are already selling successfully.

The key thing to think about with advisory/consulting is how quickly can your ideal client get a good ROI whilst working with you.

When I offer my Momentum programme to practices that are a good fit, it is an easy offer that both new and established practices snap up. We focus on making sure our clients get a huge ROI from working with us, so it is a no brainer to do so.

Here is how you could frame your offer (and how we frame ours):

'If you give me 6k and within 12 months I gave you the ability to turn that 6k into 100k would you see that as a good investment?'

The answer should always be yes, because you couldn't get an ROI like that from other investments (software for example).

Imagine you offered something along the same lines. Working with you will either make your client money or save them money (tax for example). If you can give them a 5 times return on their investment you become a great asset to that business. If you can give them more than that, then you become a no-brainer of an investment, and they should bite your hand off if they see the value.

The more money a business has, the bigger an impact you and your practice can have on it.

What I am hoping to get you to see, is that you can set yourself up for success by going for easy wins.

Keys to choosing the right ideal client:

1. Keep emotion out of it. You are choosing an ideal client based purely on whether you can get them results.

2. Can you hunt for them? You want an ideal client that you can find easily online and not have to wait for them to find you.

3. They must have money. Whilst working with startups might be exciting they often don't have the cash for advisory. Choose businesses that are established and with a good turnover.

4. Businesses want experts. Experts that understand their industry. You will be able to charge more if you niche.

Remember those numbers we went over to get a Freedom Practice?

Because you don't need thousands of clients you can be picky.

Because choosing an ideal client is about the impact you will make on them and their practice, you will be able to sell with much less resistance.

All of this points to your success. Higher revenue. Fewer clients.

How To Get Clients - The 'Old Way' c. 1995

The 'old way' was not the wrong way. It's just not the best way for the way people buy products and services nowadays.

The 'old way' of getting clients was either through referrals/word of mouth or through investing in advertising (yellow pages, radio advert etc).

It would go something like this:

>> Business Owner A needs an accountant

>> They go to the yellow pages

>> They search accountants local to them

>> They choose the accountant nearest the top with the biggest listing which is always the a firm beginning with A e.g. ABC Accounting Firm

>> They call ABC Accounting Firm and arrange a meeting

>> ABC Accounting Firm has a meeting, presents services in a long meeting

>> Convinces Business Owner A to buy from them with a special low price

Business Owner A invests in ABC Accounting Firm, but only after another couple of meetings with BDC accountants and CDE accountants. And only because ABC Accounting Firm is slightly cheaper. (All firms visited offered a special low price).

How To Get Clients - The New Way c. 2021

Potential ideal clients are now very savvy buyers. The yellow pages are no longer the go-to source to find suppliers.

Now buyers are in control of who they buy from, and what services they want to buy.

When a buyer is looking for advice around accounting/their numbers, they turn to social media platforms like Facebook or Linkedin, or they search on Google for answers.

Buyers do their own research around their pains and problems. They read blogs/articles, watch videos, listen to podcasts. They consume and learn as much as they can so they understand what their real problem is before they look for a solution.

They start with searches on Google. Or they stumble across a blog/article on Facebook or LinkedIn that peaks their interest. Or they are browsing Instagram and an advert comes up targeting them and the title is so good they click on the link.

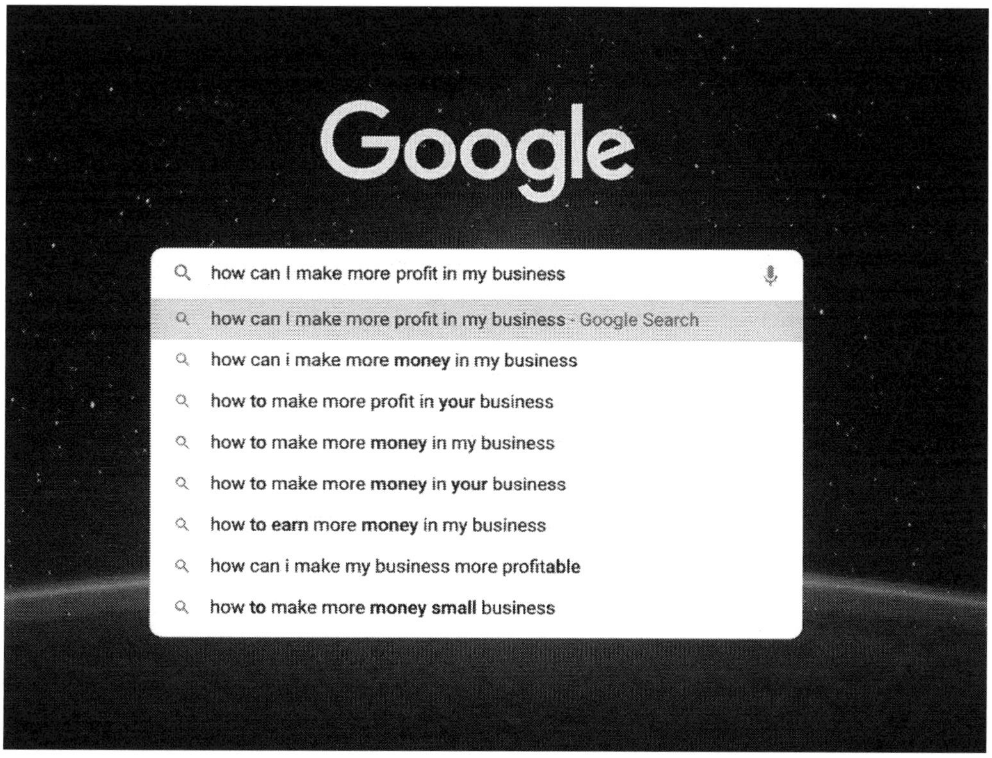

All of the actions they take start with one thing. Looking for a solution to a problem they know they have.

If a buyer knows what their problems are they initially do their own research to overcome the problem.

And it is the accounting practice that has the answers to their problem, and educates them the most around overcoming their problem that gets first dibs when it comes to selling to them.

The biggest disadvantage the accounting profession has c. 2021 is that business coaches are more marketing savvy than the typical accountant. Business coaches/consultants are scooping up all the advisory/consulting work because they are front of mind and visible to those who have problems.

These business coaches/consultants are scooping up YOUR advisory/consulting work.

And what is worse than them getting your clients? The fact that they are not able to advise around the numbers like you are. They do not have the expertise you have.

So the question becomes... How do you get the advisory/consulting work instead of the business coaches getting the work?

And the answer is simple: You don't use industry jargon, you don't speak accountanese, you don't rely on referrals, and you certainly don't sell on price.

Instead we focus on one thing. Uplevelling the profession so that all accounting practices are seen as a **VITAL asset to a business.**

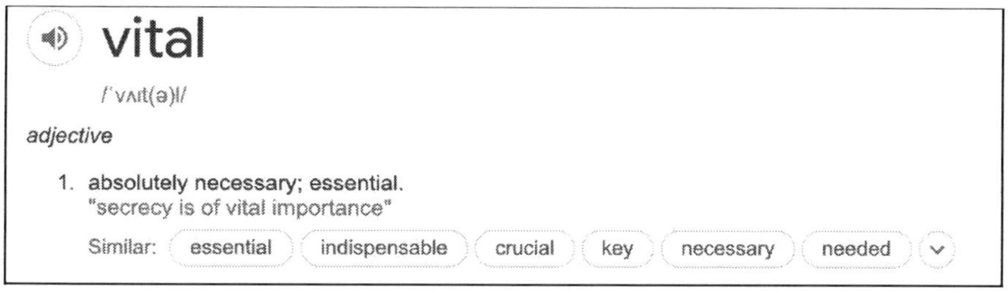

vital

/ˈvʌɪt(ə)l/

adjective

1. absolutely necessary; essential.
"secrecy is of vital importance"
Similar: essential indispensable crucial key necessary needed

Let me break this down for you. VITAL not only stands for absolutely necessary; essential, but is also an acronym describing how you need to be seen in your client's eyes.

The V stands for VALUE

You must give huge amounts of value to your prospects and your clients. Give away your best advice for free. The value you provide builds relationships, and this is key to have people buy from you on results not price.

The I stands for IMPACT

If you are seen as an accounting practice that has a mission bigger than you, people will respect that. Focusing on helping as many people in the world as possible will change the world for the better. The ripple effect kicks in, and the bigger your impact on people, businesses and the world, the more your life will change for the better.

The T stands for TRUST

No business will listen to you if they do not trust you are the expert. If you want to have clients that listen and take action on your advice you need to position you and your firm as trusted advisors. This trust will translate into respect and then your relationship with your clients will blossom into a very rewarding relationship for both parties.

The A stands for AGILE

Do you move fast when you need to? Since the start of 2020 we have seen Brexit in the UK, a new President in the USA, terrible bushfires in Australia, not to mention the global pandemic that started in 2019 and is still raging throughout the lands in 2021. Businesses have broken, far more than ever could have been conceived, they have been bleeding from the neck and some have been sinking ships.

Accountants have had to think on their feet, translate new legislation quicker than they can give the legislation a name (did anyone know what furlough was before the pandemic?) and be the most agile they have ever been. But it's only the accountants that showed their agility that thrived during the difficult times. Business owners were quick to leave accountants that did not help them during these times, and they were desperate for help. Business owners want modern and agile accountants, not the traditional accountants stuck in their ways still offering out of date advice and support.

The L stands for LUCRATIVE.

According to Google the meaning of the word lucrative is 'making a great deal of profit'. Remember earlier when I told you about how working with you should reap a positive ROI. Well this is what I am talking about here. If you can make a great deal of profit for your clients, they will no longer see you as a cost but an investment. If you are making your clients more lucrative, you will become more lucrative yourself. Funny how that works eh?

And for these reasons above you must position you and your practice as VITAL.

You must be:

- Valuable
- Impactful
- Trusted
- Agile
- Lucrative

How To Get Advisory Clients Fast

Up to now you may have been screaming at me saying 'you promised me clients Amanda, where is the bit where it teaches me sales and how to get clients'.

And my answer to you is - we have been working on the most important sale of your entire life.

> *'The most important sale in life is to sell yourself to yourself' Maxwell Maltz*

You have to believe that you can do this. You have to believe that you are the answer to a business's problem. You have to believe that what you offer is valuable. You have to believe that no one out there has your experience (which they do not because each experience is unique). You have to believe so much in yourself that you want to shout about how great you are.

If you are not 100% sold on you, then you will struggle to be able to convince your prospect that you are the answer.

Belief can take time, it is like a muscle. It grows the more you work it. I have planted the seed of belief in you and together we can grow it so you are a powerhouse.

Let's now move on to stage two where I share how to get advisory/consulting clients.

Getting Momentum

According to physics this is the equation for Momentum is:

Momentum = mass x velocity

Which basically translates to - the more you do something (mass) and the faster you do it (velocity) the more momentum you will have.

And for you and I, **MOMENTUM = PRACTICE GROWTH**

To get Momentum you need to take 4 actions, every day:

1. Hunt for your Hunting Niche® and build your connections/your audience

2. Advance the 'now' buyers from your new connections and audience into conversations

3. Farm your 'not now' buyers from your connections and audience and get them into conversations by staying front of mind (FOM)

4. Sell to those who have booked conversations with you, if they pass the audition process.

Step One - Going Hunting For Your Hunting Niche®

You have never, ever, ever had such an incredible opportunity to get in front of your ideal prospect so quickly and inexpensively as you do today. It's time to make hay whilst the sun shines.

To build a large audience of ideal prospects you need 2 things.

1. To know exactly who they are

2. To know exactly where they hang out on line

The rest is a numbers game. If your ideal prospect is on LinkedIn, then you need to build your audience on LinkedIn. If your ideal prospect is on Facebook then you need to build your audience on Facebook. If your ideal prospect is on both platforms then you need to build your audience on both platforms. Your ideal prospect may hang out on Instagram or Twitter too.

You won't know where they hang out until you know who they exactly are. So your first job before you do any marketing is to get clear on your ideal prospect.

Once you are clear you need to spend every day adding these ideal prospects to your followers and connections across the different platforms so you get known. Momentum comes when you do a few actions every day with consistency. Like asking people to connect with you on social media.

- 10 connections a day on one platform = 3,650 a year
- 20 connections a day on one platform = 7,300 a year
- 10 connections a day on two platforms = 7,300 a year
- 20 connections a day on two platforms = 14,600 a year

All these connections are ideal prospects - that is a lot of opportunities that you can have in front of you. The accountant who focuses on taking action will maximise their opportunities. You will hear me say this time and time again, marketing is just math, with a smiging of psychology for good measure.

Step Two - Advancing Your New Audience/Connections

Once you are consistently building an audience of your ideal prospects you need to engage with them and advance them into conversations to see if they are a potential client.

To do this you simply need to understand 2 things:

1. Their biggest challenge/questions they are asking themselves

2. The answers to this challenge/these questions

To initially engage your ideal prospects you need to give them the answers to their challenge/questions. You do this in the form of content marketing - ebooks, books, videos, blogs, articles, podcasts. This is often the first contact you will have with your audience and this content needs to illuminate/highlight their problems so they see your content as hugely valuable.

But engaging with them isn't enough. Engagement on social media does not get you clients. The only way you can get a client is through having some kind of conversation. Content peaks interest. But you need conversation starters to get sales calls in the diary.

Starting Conversations With Your New Audience

Once we have got your new ideal prospects to engage with your content we need to advance them by starting some kind of dialogue with them. Either through messaging on social media, or getting them to book calls in your diary using an online scheduler.

There is a reason I get an average of 2 prospects a day becoming clients of Momentum, Get Clients Now or The Content Lounge.

And that reason is quite simple - I start conversations with 50 people a day or more (25 conversations on Facebook, and 25 on Linkedin).

- The content I create leads to engagement.
- The engagement enables me to start conversations.
- And the conversations I have lead to clients.

More Content = More Engagement

More Engagement = More Conversations

More Conversations = More Clients

Have you heard me mention the math word? Let me repeat it for you in case you missed it... it's just math, with a smidgen of psychology for good measure.

Step Three - Farming Your Audience/Database

The Value Of Unconverted Leads

When you start marketing in earnest you will find that you will generate an audience where not all of them will become clients. Some of them will become clients fast (within 90 days). Some will close slow (within 2 years). And some will never become clients.

Those who do not become clients fast can leave you frustrated and feel like you could have wasted your time, but that is a pretty short sighted view.

If you have done your homework and understood your target market the audience you have spent time building will be interested in what you have to offer at some point.

One of the greatest assets your new or established practice will ever have is the bunch of email subscribers (prospect database) that you will build for your practice. This database will be eager and waiting for more valuable help if you are getting your content marketing right. If done right you will nurture your database and stay front of mind, so that when they are ready to buy the only choice is you.

A survey was carried out by a company that handles enquiries on an enterprise level. This company sends out a 'did you buy' survey asking people if they bought the product they originally enquired about.

This is what they discovered:

People who enquired about a service usually bought it within 18 months - 2 years. This doesn't mean they bought it from the company they originally enquired from, it just means they bought that service.

Of the people who bought in that 18 month - 2 year period, only 10% did so in the first 90 days. This means 90% of the value of leads you generate today is 90 days or more away.

'90% of the value of leads you generate today is 90 days or more away'

Going Farming

Your advancing strategy will hook your audience who are interested in your offer now or in the next 90 days. Your farming strategy will keep your audience who are 'not now buyers' in your world until they become 'now buyers'.

Just like with agriculture you plant seeds and then farm the crops when they are ready, we do the same with our audience.

When you go hunting for your ideal prospect, and connect with them across social media you are planting seeds, and starting a relationship.

But it doesn't stop there. You need to water and feed the relationship, nurture it and bring value to it. You need to help the relationship grow. This is farming.

If you fail to continue to feed the relationship then this is when your ideal prospect turns to others for help. They will turn to others because you have failed to keep them engaged where your competitors have not. If your competitors provide more value than you they will turn to them.

This is why content marketing is so powerful. Content marketing enables you to position your practice as VITAL, so when the time is right you are the practice they come to. Content marketing enables you to farm your audience. Reap the seeds you have sown over time.

'Content marketing keeps you front of mind, feeds your relationships with your ideal clients, and gives them huge value in the process.'

During this stage you want your 'not now' prospects thinking of you not your competitors. This way when they become a 'now' prospect they turn to you for the service.

Content marketing can often be too time consuming, or feel like way too hard work and difficult for many accountants. The mere thought of having to write an article, post on social media or record a video can feel overwhelming.

The effort of content marketing does not equal the reward, or so it may have seemed before I shared the true value of it with you.

By reading this book you have been informed about the 10% of 'now buyers'. If you continue not to embrace content marketing you will absolutely miss out on the 90% of 'not now but later' buyers.

The good news is content marketing doesn't have to be overthought. Content marketing is for you to stay front of mind. You don't have to be the next Stephen King or James Patterson to have your content work for you. You don't have to be creative. And you don't have to experiment with it.

What your content marketing must do:

Illuminate - your content marketing must illuminate your prospects problems, and interrupt their day enough to grab their attention. All of the focus is on your client and the pain they have.

Educate - once your ideal client has had their problems/pain highlighted and they are aware they need to find a solution, your educational content needs help them feel confident that they can overcome their pain. This content is focused on a solution for your prospect.

Convert - at this stage your ideal prospect is pretty savvy, and understands what they are looking for. Content at this stage should start to be more about you, your practice, and past clients that are winning by working with you.

These three stages of content creation I call the Traffic Light Method™, it takes a client from RED (stuck) to AMBER (getting ready to move) to GREEN (where they are good to go and take action).

One of the things I realised many years ago is the power of 'out contenting competitors'.

Quantity Over Quality

Whilst quality of content is important, quality does not trump quantity and consistency.

The accountant who posts on social media every day, and creates a blog 2-3 times a week and sends out a newsletter to their database every week, will get more clients than the accountant who writes one highly thought out and overproofed 1500 word article every month.

This is why I created The Content Lounge for accountants, outsourced CFOs and Bookkeepers. A place where you can get all the content you need, without the need to experiment or be creative. You can find out more details at https://oompf.global/thecontentlounge

Step Four - Sales

To make a sale, you have to ask for the sale.

Be honest with yourself. How many sales conversations have you had this week, month, year? Do you even know?

Many of you come to me with a common problem - desperate for new and better clients in their practice, and the need for dramatically improving their profits. You have empty pipelines, no sales meetings scheduled, and no hope of booking any on the horizon.

The lack of sales conversations booked in the diary triggers the Universal Law Of Need.

What Happens When You Have No Sales Calls In The Diary?

When you do not have enquiries, or a diary full of sales calls you can feel desperate for a sale. You end up 'wanting' and 'needing' clients. If you do get an enquiry your probability of discounting just to get the sale increases. The ability to objectively decide if a client is a good client or Vampire client also goes out the window.

This desperation destroys your freedom.

THE SALES FUNNEL

(Hunting, Advancing, Farming And Sales)

The act of hunting, advancing, farming and holding sales calls is a very simple outline of a sales funnel.

What is a sales funnel? Sales funnels are really just marketing speak for your audience's journey from cold to hot lead and beyond. A funnel is not a tool. It is a philosophy/strategy for how to move people from not knowing you to becoming a paid client.

Sometimes a sales funnel is easy and fast, for example '*they see an ad, and buy a thing*'.

Sometimes it is slow and elongated because a lot of warming up of the relationship needs to happen.

You may wonder why a sales funnel is needed in your practice, as you have relied quite nicely on referrals. However, a sales funnel gives you more control over what clients you onboard into your practice and actions you want your audience to take to get to this point. A sales funnel enables you to test and measure your marketing and eliminate the stuff that just doesn't work.

I do see a lot of practice owners make mistakes when it comes to their sales funnel.

Mistakes include:

- Not being clear on your Hunting Niche® and trying to market to everyone
- Not having a clear message to differentiate your practice
- No calls to action, or worse - too many calls to action
- No follow up with leads
- Not having an offer than transforms businesses (compliance only)
- Being too salesy

And these mistakes cause a bunch of problems. Most importantly you can spend way too much time and money for way too little results.

I know what you might be thinking. This sounds like marketing snake oil, and is just a tactic that marketers use to get money from you.

Well you are right, and you are wrong. Because sales funnels can be a money pit, especially if you plough money into Facebook advertising without testing the funnel organically first.

But conversely, when done right they can be the easiest and most rewarding marketing strategy you could ever carry out.

The kind of sales funnel I am sharing with you today isn't a slimy sales tactic. It's about providing value at the right time to the right person with the right message.

A sales funnel is a powerful way to generate and nurture leads:

→ **Hunting** is the start of your sales funnel. It builds your audience.

→ **Advancing** is moving the now buyers to become a lead.

→ **Farming** is nurturing the lead to become a prospect.

→ **Sales** takes your prospect and turns them into a client.

Let me share with you an example of a simple sales funnel for an accountant that has a hunting niche of 'dentists'.

Hunting: You build your audience of dentists on LinkedIn connecting with ideal clients every day.

Advancing: You get the now buyers to raise their hands by getting them to do one of two things.

Either a) download your ebook/come to a webinar Or b) offer to jump on a call with them (this will be snapped up by only a few people, as 90% of your audience will take up to 2 years to be interested in your services).

Farming: For those who are not 'now buyers' but 'later buyers' you focus on staying front of mind (FOM) and building credibility. Here you can shower them with a huge amount of valuable content and send them a weekly email, or invite them into a Facebook Group for example. The aim is to leverage content marketing to farm the seeds you planted when you went hunting.

Sales: Getting calls booked into the diary and having sales conversations. This part of the sales funnel is self explanatory, although it must be done in the right way to maximize conversion rates and secure the higher value clients.

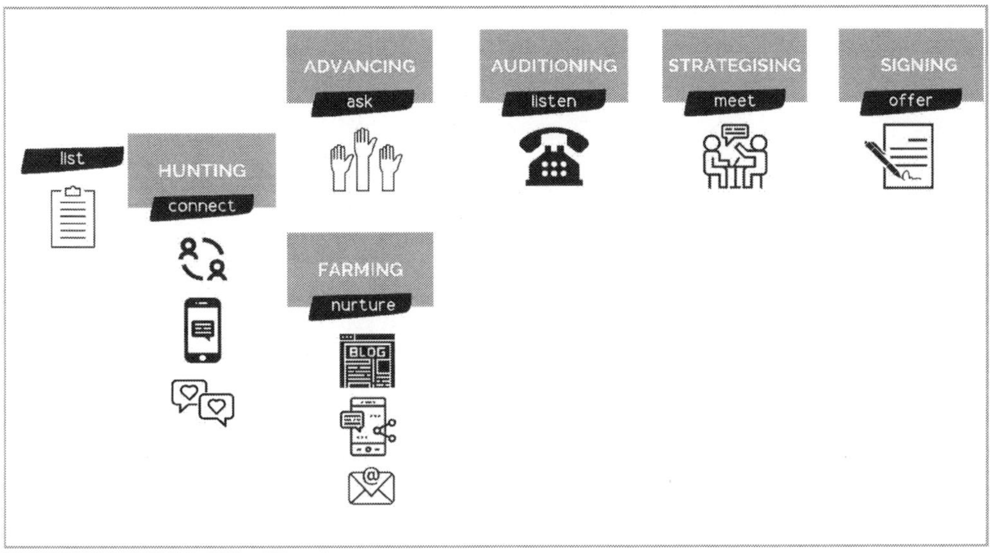

There is a huge opportunity available for those who put a sales funnel into their practice. These opportunities include:

- Predictable leadflow
- Only speaking to ideal clients and not potential vampires
- The ability to turn your leadflow on or off
- Marketing that can be tested (anything that isn't working can be cut fast)
- The ability to build relationships with prospects
- The advantage of scooping up all prospects so they buy from you not your competitors
- An automated marketing system that leverages your time...

The list goes on and on..

You are only one sales funnel away from creating your Freedom Practice.

Kick Starting Conversations

To make the sale you have to ask for the sale.

And to ask for the sale you need to have a conversation.

And to have a conversation you need people to raise their hand and show they are interested in having one.

Three things happen when you focus on getting conversations in the diary:

1. Your marketing becomes purposeful. Which makes it worthwhile.
2. You talk to more people, which means you have more opportunities to offer your services.
3. You make more offers which means you make more sales.

Booking conversations in the diary isn't about having chit-chats with people. It's about having high quality meetings, and is the most underappreciated opportunity practice owners have.

Trying to get excited about appointment setting can be hard. But here is the thing. You can't win the deal if no one is willing to talk to you.

Appointment Setting Hack

The key to getting more appointments in the diary is actually quite simple.

Get people to raise their hand to show they are interested in your offer.

I am not talking about getting people to raise their hand because they want management accounts, or their tax returns done. I am talking about something bigger:

That bigger thing is overcoming their problems and helping them achieve their dreams and aspirations.

Once people have raised their hand in interest, then you can focus on seeing if they are a good fit and if you can help them.

Getting them to raise their hand can be as easy as this simple post on your chosen social media channel or you can adapt slightly to send via your email marketing:

'I am looking for 3 creative agencies who want to increase their profits significantly over the next 90 days. If this sounds like you comment PROFITS below'

What this post does is focus on the 'now buyers' that are ready to buy.

You are asking your audience to self select that they are interested in your offer. Once they have expressed their interest you can then reach out and book a conversation.

Let's dissect why this post is so powerful.

1. It speaks to a Hunting Niche®. In this case, creative agencies.

2. It clearly explains your offer. In this case, more profit.

3. It clearly gives a timeline. In this case, 90 days.

4. It includes a Call To Action. In this case 'comment below'.

This kind of update is a great appointment setting hack. It will enable you to advance people into conversations, and you will make more sales.

The 3 Call Sales Process

Here's the problem. When you hold sales calls/meetings, and you get to the point where you are about to ask for the sale, there is a whole bunch of pressure.

There is pressure on you to close the sale and get the money in the bank.

The pressure is also on the prospect. They feel like they are being sold to and before you have even started the meeting they are defensive and looking for a deal.

This pressure is not good for you, and it's not good for the prospect. It's an icky start to a working relationship.

If sales calls = pressure, then we have to reframe the situation so that it becomes an enjoyable experience for both parties. Not only enjoyable but hugely beneficial despite there being a sale or not.

And instead of you working hard to make a sale, how about you putting yourself in the judge's seat, and deciding if they are a good fit or not. Just like Simon Cowell does in Britains Got Talent or The X Factor.

Like Simon does, you too can decide if your prospect can advance onto the next stage of the audition, or if they are going home and are not a good fit.

How about you being in the power position, instead of the begging position?

When you master the sales process well, your prospects will want to buy from you. You won't have to give them the hard sell. There will be no snake oil or closing questions, and your client will want to sign up without questioning you on price.

If you do this right you will find you will sign up 80% or more of your prospects, and they will be high value clients. Not the Vampire clients you have currently been attracting and having to sell to.

We teach a 3 step sales process in our Momentum programme. And it goes like this:

- Audition Call (Listen to the prospect)
- Strategy Session (Have an in-depth meeting with an ideal client)
- Proposal Session (Present your offer and get a high value client)

Step 1. The Audition Call. This is a short call, just 10 minutes long and in it you put on your Simon Cowell pants. It is where you ask questions and get answers. It is where you assess if they are a good fit and get through to the next round, or get sent away with no hope of working with you.

During this call you do not discuss how you work with people, a solution to their problems or coach them.

All you do is see if they are a potential ideal client. Do they have a problem you can overcome, and can they afford you? Are they a fit, or a no fit?

If they pass the audition then you book in a meeting for the next round.

Step 2. The Strategy Session. This call is a little longer. 30 minutes of you getting super clear on what their business is like now, what they want it to be like, and the gap that they have of things that are missing. At the end of this call you will be able to have a deep understanding of what they need and give a brief outline of how you can help them.

During this call you do not have to tell them how much it costs to work with you. You can give a ballpark estimate, but not a definitive answer. If both of you feel comfortable at the end of this session, then they can agree in principle that they want to work with you. And you can agree to create a proposal after the strategy session.

Some of you may use proposal software. If this is the case you may move to the proposal stage during the strategy session call and share the deliverables and the cost for the deliverables. If this is the case you will have to be ready to overcome any price objections, and if things go well be ready to sign them up.

If you do not use proposal software then you must continue on the 3 Call Sales Process. At the point where they say that they want to work with you in principle, you organise a subsequent call (call 3) into both your diaries to talk through the proposal.

Step 3. The Proposal Session. The Proposal Session is no longer a two way conversation. It is you presenting your offer/proposal (we suggest via PowerPoint/Google Slides). As you present your offer/proposal you recap on your clients pains and how your service offering is the solution to these pains. The proposal session is for you to talk about you, and reconfirm how you are their solution to their pains.

During this session you take your potential client on a journey - there are six steps that you take your prospect through, so that at the end of the presentation they excitedly sign on the dotted line.

This process may take 30-45 minutes or more. At the end of the call you will have a client, or not. And if you do not have a client then something went wrong in the Audition Call or Strategy Session, because these two calls are there to set up the sale, and ensure you get the high value client.

Running your sales process using this 3 Call Sales Process has an advantage over the traditional one stop meeting and then sending a proposal via email scenario.

That advantage is:

CONTROL

You control the process at all times. You control whether you want to work with the prospect, and you control how and when the prospect buys.

It's important not to rush this process. It may take you 7-14 days to get the client to sign a contract/letter of engagement, but psychologically it builds a very strong relationship between you and the potential client.

During this process you will know for certain if they will become a client or not and you will no longer be left in limbo waiting for people to sign.

No more hoping.

You will have complete control over the whole process. From auditioning to signing on the dotted line, you decide the outcomes.

The Law Of Replacement

The Law Of Replacement is a concept that teaches you something very valuable. It teaches you that you must replace opportunities that are no longer there. In this case I am talking about prospective clients that fall out of your pipeline - either by becoming a client or by not being a good fit.

Let's look at the math behind the Law Of Replacement.

You have 10 sales calls booked in your diary.

Out of these 10 sales calls, one becomes a client. 9 do not.

Does this mean you need to get 1 more call in the diary to make another sale? No.

10 people have dropped out of your sales pipeline, which means to make a sale you need to book in another 10 sales calls.

The Law Of Replacement has to also take into consideration the Law Of Averages.

It teaches you two things.

1. The importance of understanding how many prospects you need in your pipeline for you to get a high value advisory client.

2. It shows you how critical it is to focus on finding new prospects as your pipeline depletes.

So let's recap on a few key principles.

1. You must implement a sales funnel in your business. There is a new way to do marketing.

2. You need to run a 3 call sales process when it comes to selling high value advisory services.

3. You need to invoke the Law Of Replacement when it comes to getting sales calls in the diary.

Once you start to implement a strategic marketing and sales process in your practice as I have outlined, you will create a freedom based advisory/consulting business.

PART THREE - HOW TO SCALE YOUR PRACTICE

I could leave you now and you will have got huge value from the Practice Growth Superpowers book. I have shown you the importance of advisory, and how to create a Freedom Practice you truly desire, leveraging sales and marketing superpowers.

But if I leave you now I will be doing you a disservice. I have a couple more superpowers up my sleeve that I really want to share with you.

These superpowers I share with you today have changed my life and my clients' lives. They have taken me from 20k-30k months to 100k months and more. And they can do the same for you.

However, they may require you to really shift your thinking. The information I share in the following pages, if implemented, will need you to act differently to how a practice owner might have traditionally acted.

I previously mentioned the importance of being agile. Here is your first chance to embrace it.

The biggest problem that most accountants and outsourced CFOs have is not the systems/apps they need to integrate into the practice, or the team they need to hire. The biggest problem is the business model they bought into when they started out.

The traditional business model says: do compliance for all clients, do year end tax, do the personal tax of the business owner, offer advice and help people 1:1. You and the client. In a room. Face to face. Time for money. Advisory.

Your effort and your time.

Limited effort. Limited time.

It's just you, helping a handful of clients, 20, 50 of them. 100 at most if you offer and deliver your own advisory services.

And if you are offering only compliance you have to have hundreds of clients, and are working hundreds of hours to serve them with a large team to support you.

This model is broken.

And not many practice owners know how to fix it or change their situation.

They say 'this is as good as it gets', and settle for a mediocre practice, with mediocre profits, and little to no time in their life.

Or they try and create a faster horse, rather than taking a step forward into the 21st century and creating a Formula 1 motor car.

Today I want to share a different option and give you the opportunity to change your advisory/consulting delivery model. This model requires a new way of thinking. It requires you to be agile in your delivery. And it requires you to spend some time delving into unpacking your intellectual property.

This new model consists of two parts.

1. A scalable service **OFFERING**.

And

2. A scalable service **DELIVERY**.

You can have 1 without 2, but you cannot have 2 without 1.

Intrigued?

Let's dive in...

1. A Scalable Service Offering

It is my life's mission to uplevel the accountancy profession for the better. You might be surprised to know marketing and sales are not why I do what I do. I do what I do because I have been called to help others. I love teaching and inspiring and motivating people. I love making an impact. I want to create ripples that spread far and wide. In fact I want to create huge freaking waves that accountants and CFOs can ride to create their own practice freedom. Freedom is a right that everybody has, and most people struggle to find/get it. Which is why I want to help as many people as possible to achieve it.

There is a lot of information out there that is wrong when it comes to growing a practice. There is often too much focus on telling practice owners that they must do their own content marketing. They must learn how to write blogs and articles. There is too much focus on getting the software set up before the practice owner even has any clients to use the software! There is too much focus on pricing services before they have even practiced delivering services and know what their focus will be.

This is a classic example of putting the cart before the horse. And stops practices dead in their tracks and unable to move forward.

Your job as a practice owner is to do one thing. Get and keep a client.

Your job if you want to create a Freedom Practice is to get and keep better clients whilst offering leveraged advisory/consultancy and having huge profits.

Your Offer

The most important strategy I have ever taught to consultants and advisors, the one which has made the biggest difference on income, time, freedom and impact is showing how to build an effective and profitable Signature System.

I'll detail what a Signature System is in a minute, but first let me explain why having a Signature System is essential and how it will transform both your business and your life.

Imagine if you could:

⇨ Have a rock-solid methodology for packaging your service offering so it provides a powerful transformation for your client.

⇨ Never have to charge by the hour for your services again, because there will be so much value when you share your offering, people will never question you on price.

⇨ Be known for a specific service and have people recommending working with you because of your transformational results, and not just being recommended for 'being an accountant'.

⇨ Get your work out to a wider audience, so you can make more money and have more impact.

⇨ Attract high-value clients that never question you on price but in fact throw money at you (even if you don't do any compliance work for them).

Sound good? Well, this is what a Signature System can do for you and your practice.

Let me share with you what a Signature System is not.

✗ A Signature System is not putting together a package of 5/10 advisory sessions and then selling them at a discount. All this does is lower the hourly rate you earn.

✗ A Signature System is not creating a low ticket offer that you package and sell online as a 'do-it-yourself' offer. This just means you have to reach thousands of people in order to make real income.

A Signature System is productising your services to de-commoditise your practice. It:

✓ Is your hard earned experience unpacked into a step by step methodology that transforms your clients life and business.

✓ Is the backbone to all your service offerings and can be sold as advisory, as coaching/consulting programmes, as an online course, as a mastermind.

✓ Can give you some great marketing ideas and assets, taking away the need to be creative and experiment, and giving you a clear outline for the content you can create for your marketing.

✓ Can be used at any stage in the buyer's journey to highlight problems your clients/prospects have, through to converting them into a client, and then delivery of the service outlined in the Signature System.

Imagine for a minute what your practice would be like if you no longer had to stress about your service offering, but instead had a repeatable system that transformed lives. A way of working that overcomes specific problems and leverages your hard earned learnings.

Imagine you have productised your services to de-commoditise your practice.

This is the only way to future proof your practice. The world is eventually going to be full of accountants, bookkeepers, outsourced CFOs and financial consultants/strategists offering advisory.

Every day there is a new piece of software that claims to support accountants to deliver better advisory services in an easy way.

These new and exciting software packages are enabling those with little or no advisory experience to compete with those who have years of experience.

Not to mention the fact that business coaches are also offering advisory services to your clients. And they often have no qualifications or previous business experience.

So you have to think differently to stay ahead of the curve. It is not enough to be digital, it is not enough to be an advisor...

Right now you need to think like a Grandmaster chess player.

In chess a Grandmaster is the most difficult ranking to earn. They have won more games (points) than their opponents.

Despite what you might imagine, Grandmasters do not have a higher IQ than other chess players. They just study and master the game. They focus on honing their strategy to out think their competition.

Thinking like a Grandmaster is about knowing the end game. Knowing the end game enables you to put a winning strategy together so that you get the high value clients. When you understand your clients fears and problems you can create a strategy for your clients so they can win their end game too. Your Signature System enables you to articulate your strategy to your prospects so that they can see how they too can win the game of chess.

The moment you create a Signature System you have productised your practice and will start to reap the benefits. Talking to existing clients about your new offering, or having conversations with prospects and using your Signature System to differentiate your practice, will see an instant uplift in your profits and income. It will also future proof your practice, and if you do want to sell, you will have strong Intellectual Property (IP) that increases your value.

Your Offering - How Do You Create A Signature System?

A Signature System is a structured way to move someone from the pain they are in right now, through to where they desperately want to be.

It's like the mountain climber that wants to be at the top of the mountain. Where is he now? Right now he is at basecamp.

Where does he want to be? He wants to be at the summit.

How does he get there? Using a guide that takes him safely to the top. This guide will take him through key milestones and ensure he doesn't veer off course to reach his goals/get him to the top.

Building Your Signature System

Your Signature System is a combination of two things. 1. What your client wants/needs and 2. What you know (experience and insights).

Then these two things are combined to bring a guaranteed outcome.

Your Signature System is a step by step methodology that takes your clients from A-B (a problem to a promise), covering certain milestones along the way.

Kristina Coluccia from Woodburn Advisors & Accountants has been my client for a couple of years.

During our time together she has grown a strong prospect database of over 15,000 subscribers, run monthly webinar series, grown her LinkedIn account and is getting clients on a monthly basis from her social media, clients paying her £2k a month or more.

One of the key factors in being able to price her services at such a high level is that she is able to articulate her true value. She has a 9 step methodology (Signature System) which she uses in all her marketing and in the delivery of her services.

Since developing this Signature System in 2020 (The China Roadmap™) she has gone on to develop other Signature Systems that sit underneath this one.

You will see that by unpacking her intellectual property and experience, and packaging up this IP and experience into a Signature System, she has created a transformational service. By turning the accounting/advisory services into a powerful model she has productised it.

And by productising her offering she has decommoditised her practice.

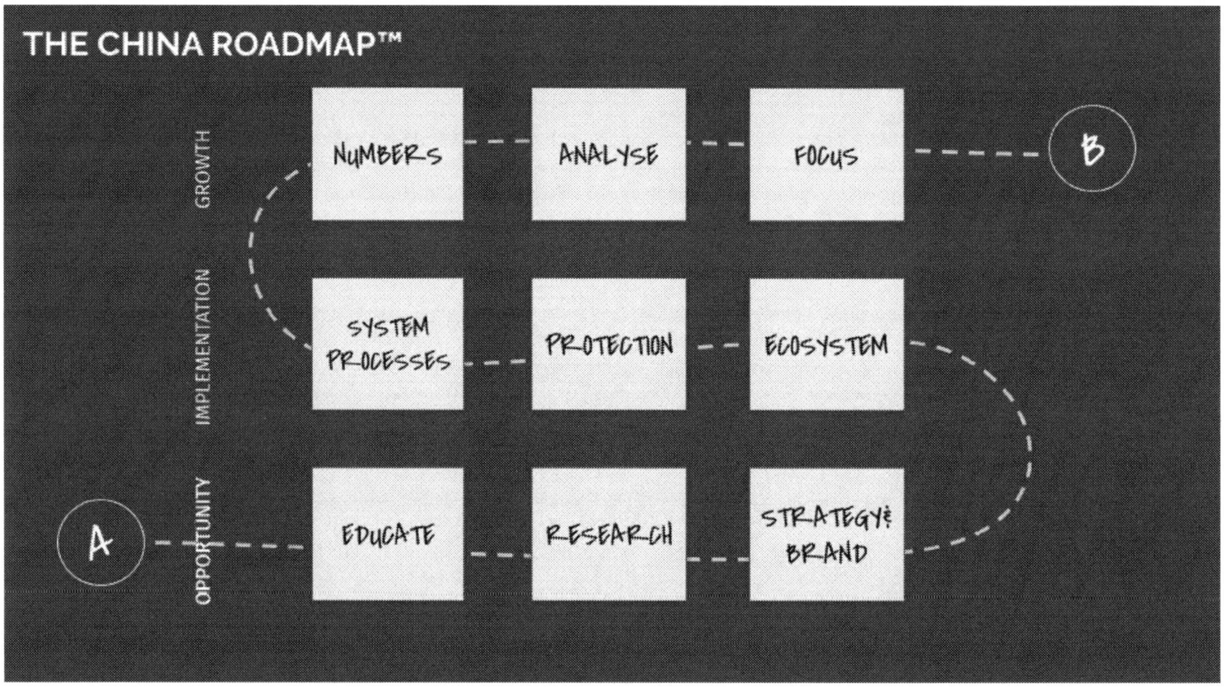

Kristina has also given her and her practice service delivery options. She can sell one strategy within the Signature System, or The China Roadmap as a whole transformational system. What she does not ever sell though, is time.

And this is where your journey with creating a Signature System starts.

Now we can dive into step 2. Delivering Your Signature System (Offer)

2. A Scalable Service Delivery

Traditionally accountants, outsourced CFOs and financial coaches have offered one thing. 'Done-for-you' accounting services.

If you look up the word accountant in the dictionary this is what comes up : a person whose job is to keep, inspect, and analyse financial accounts.

But times are changing. You are more than your traditional meaning. You are in a prime position to not only package up your offering, but deliver it in a whole new way. In a digital way, a way that leverages time, effort and gets great results for your clients. A way that gives you more profits and has you working way less hours.

Switching To The New Model.

As you will have seen there is a common theme throughout this book. And that theme is the 'old way' of doing things, and the 'new way'.

And the same goes for the way you deliver your services. There is the traditional way of running your accounting practice, which is the 'done for you' model or 1:1 advisory/consulting and then there is a new model. Which I call the Hybrid Model. The Hybrid Model is where you have a mixture of 'Done-for-you' Compliance and a leveraged advisory model of online/group coaching/advisory. This really leverages your time and will make you far more money with ease.

The new model of delivery, the Hybrid Model, refers to a way of delivering a transformation for your clients, without having to execute your services in the flesh. Instead you deliver the advisory virtually through digital training videos, programmes or mastermind groups.

Getting your Signature System mapped out and starting to deliver it 1:1 enables you to test the water when it comes to your advisory/consulting. However there is nothing stopping you from leveraging most of your advisory by offering it in a group face to face or via digital means.

You can deliver the same advice, and the same result by leveraging machines and technology. A lot of people think 'oh I won't be able to deliver that as digital training, or I won't be able to teach it with step by step instructions'. Yes you will be able to. Believe me, there are way more complicated things in the world than delivering advice, and these things have been turned into a repeatable process.

It's just a mindset shift.

Once you start to observe the work you do, the advice you give and the fact that much of what you say is repeated to every client, you can see that your time can be leveraged.

Our two flagship programmes - Momentum and Get Clients Now are a great example of leveraging advisory through the Hybrid Model. Each of the programmes have 'done-for-you' pre-written social media content and articles that you can plug and play. Some of each programme is pre-recorded training that enables you to take the strategy and bespoke it to fit your practice. And some of it is group advisory, answering questions and helping our clients move forward, faster.

I help accountants, outsourced CFOs and financial coaches from all over the world, whilst sat in my apartment overlooking the sea. I run my business from a laptop, I have upgraded my microphone to a Yeti Mic, and I teach my clients by drawing models and ideas on my iPad.

I have a Freedom Practice and live a life I have purposely created from my deepest dreams and desires. My days are spent waking up early - I drink tea in bed watching the tide go out or come in depending on where the moon is located in the sky. I then take a morning stroll with my puppy along the seafront, soaking up the eclectic atmosphere and stopping to pick up a steaming cup of coffee from the highly acclaimed Goat Ledge Cafe, I sometimes sit a while, continue to people watch as I start my day in a calm and relaxed environment (unless it's blowing a storm, which I have to admit happens quite a lot in the winter months). I then stroll back to our apartment, take off my shoes, pour myself another coffee and start my day of sharing practice growth superpowers with my clients and my online audience.

Regardless of their knowledge or expertise I show accountants and outsourced CFOs how to grow and scale an advisory/consulting practice, get clients and make more profits - often from scratch.

This model enables me to work 8 hours a week with my clients serving over 500 clients at a time, with a small team helping me with the admin and marketing, whilst making 7 figures in our practice. Now that is a great practice model. And it is a model and way of life that you can have too. (Although you do not need to get a puppy or live by the sea unless you want to).

Let's see what this model looks like in an accounting practice.

Imagine you offer the Hybrid Model. A practice of two elements, joined through a common theme.

Element 1 - Compliance

Element number one is your compliance offering. This in itself is scalable if highly automated or outsourced. It is not highly profitable though.

Being compliant is essential for all businesses so it's a no-brainer offering for most practices. And if you do offer compliance it can aid in your advisory knowledge for each business.

Element 2 - Leveraged Advisory

Before I jump into more details on leveraged advisory, let's recap on the 'old way' of advisory. Advisory the 'old way' is a bottleneck for your practice and is rarely truly scalable. It relies on those with the most knowledge to show up (often just you) and spend their time (sometimes 1-3 hours per client on a monthly, quarterly or yearly basis) and put a price on their (your) advice.

Advisory is all about advising around the numbers and interpreting them. It's data driven, sprinkled with the advisor's business knowledge.

Two things come into play with the 'old way'. Not enough time in the day to offer it to many people, and not a leverageable or scalable model. If you want to scale you are reliant on more advisors, and good advisors cost lots of money. And spending a lot of money on a team of good advisors can drive profits down.

So let's look at the alternative.

LEVERAGED ADVISORY

The scalable and leverageable model.

The model that produces a transformation to your clients, It is the most efficient and effective way to make an impact on the world and your world.

When I started being an advisor/consultant I realised how inefficient it was. Working 1:1 with people, having meetings cancelled because my clients were too busy to show up for calls/meetings, giving the same advice for 8 hours a day to 8 different people on a 1:1 basis. It drove me crazy. Over time I was able to turn this 1:1 consulting/advisory offering into digital video training, group coaching/consulting structures, supportive online groups, recorded calls, and automated delivery. I created a leveraged advisory/consulting model.

The leveraged advisory that I now deliver is a machine that gives me time to really focus on one thing. Getting clients results.

Here is a cool quote from Henry Ford:

> *'Man minus the machine is a slave. Man plus the machine is a free man.'*

Henry Ford is the man that brought motorcars to the world. Before that people were doing things the traditional way, using their own legs to get around, or using a horse and cart and saving their legs from doing the hard work. It could take days and months to travel anywhere.

We take it for granted now, but if Henry Ford had just listened to the world crying out for faster horses we wouldn't have cars. But instead Henry Ford said, 'man plus machine'.

And this is what I am saying to you. The traditional model of advisory works. It gets your clients from A-B. Just like horses got us from A-B. Slow and clunky.

But leveraged/digital delivery embraces the man plus machine method. It gives you freedom, wealth, and can be a lot of fun.

Now let's talk about some of the different models of a digital/leveraged consulting/advisory model. I am sure you have seen lots of people doing a variety of different delivery models.

Maybe you have experienced digital or leveraged advisory/consulting yourself?

Model One

A Short Group Advisory/Consulting Programme. It can be a live consulting/advisory programme, where you gather a number of people in one go and work with them over a set period of time (say 6-12 weeks). It's done via live webinars, you can have a supporting facebook group etc. This model is great, but doesn't give you MRR (Monthly Recurring Revenue). The investment for courses like this can be from £200 - £6000 or more, depending on the transformation clients receive.

Model Two

A Never Ending Evergreen Group Advisory/Consulting Programme. You help people with no fixed start time or end time. It is always available to join and you have pre-recorded training your clients can follow, with supporting calls to help your clients move the needle faster, and get clarity. This is a model that works well for your accounting/CFO practice because when you take on a client the offer can always include the evergreen training/advisory and will give you a strong MRR (Monthly Recurring Revenue).

The investment for courses like this can be £200 a month to £5000 a month, again depending on the offering and the transformation for your clients.

Model Three

The Mastermind Group Model. This is not quite as scalable as the evergreen model as you will be limited with the numbers you can have in each cohort. But it does enable you to offer advisory without having to be an advisor.

This might sound strange so let me explain.

A mastermind is a group of peers who regularly meet (either in person or online) in order to give each other advice, support and guidance. The ultimate goal of a mastermind is to help members overcome complex and difficult business challenges and gain the experience of others in the room.

The mastermind groups tend to be smaller, 8 people or less, and the person organising/running the mastermind is facilitating the room, but not having to be the primary advisor in the room. It's a group effort. Masterminds can also have educational presentations, from either those in the room or outside experts. This is a great place to start if you haven't been an advisor before. It enables you to leverage your time and bring in a highly profitable revenue stream, with very little preparation time.

The investment for a mastermind can be from £50 a month to £1000 a month or more, again depending on the calibre of the people in the room and your ability to sell the concept.

So let's look at these as possible revenue streams for your advisory/consulting practice.

6-12 Week Programme Model (£200 - £6000 per member)

50 people a year take your programme

£10,000 - £300,000 income per year

Evergreen Model £200- £5,000 a month (£2400 to £60,000 a year)

50 people a year join the programme and stay for an average of 2 years.

Year one £120,000 - £3million

Year two £240,000 - £6million

Year three £240,000 - £6 million

Mastermind Group Model £50-£1,000 a month (£600-£12,000 a year)

Limited scalability because it is limited to 8 members, but let's say you run 3 Masterminds a year

£14,400 - £288,000 income per year

Which Model Is The Right One For You?

There are a few factors to determine the right model for you. These factors include your advisory experience, your time available to build training, and the profit you want to make from your leveraged advisory offering.

What I can confidently say is that one of these models is right for your practice, and it will be your mindset and confidence that will determine which you choose and the price you charge.

Ask yourself, do you want a faster horse, or do you want to turn your practice into a machine?

The Opportunity

Imagine having a rotten backache. This backache starts as a nagging pain for a few days, and you assume it's because you slept in a funny position. . After a few days you go numb to the pain and whilst it's weeks down the line and the backache is still there, you adapt so you can still function in your day to day activities.

Eventually it gets so bad that the nagging pain becomes chronic pain. The pain of your back is affecting your family and friends because you are grumpy and frustrated every day. You think you are coping fine, but those around you not only see your pain, but are feeling the stress you are going through. So after your wife/husband gives you an ultimatum you go to a chiropractor for help.

The chiropractor asks you some questions, looks at your back, and after diagnosing why the pain is occuring they tell you how to solve your pain in a way that will give you your life back - less stress, all that pain gone forever, and fun with the family.

However, you switch back to your 'it's ok it will go away on its own' default, and decide not to change your situation or work with the chiropractor to fix your back.

I see this so often when practice owners come to me for help, except the pain isn't from backache, it's from a broken model in their practice. And this broken model is giving them stress, and makes them grouchy. I see practice owners think that if they keep on doing what they have always done their situation will change.

But the truth is it doesn't.

And it won't if no action is taken.

Much of the accountancy profession is focused on optimising the broken model; trying new software apps, hiring more team members, engaging mentors that show how to get more clients (often through referrals alone), and how to price and offer traditional advisory.

The problem with this is a whole profession of faster horses, whilst your competitors, who are mostly business coaches, are zooming past you in their motor cars, overtaking you and winning the race to impact and freedom.

But note that I said much of the accountancy profession is focused on optimising the broken model, not all of the accountancy profession. Some of you are seeing the value in leveraged advisory. People like Bob Gaveraux from Gavereaux & Associates and Annette Ferguson from Annette and Co. Accountants like Hetty, Ben, Carl, Mary-Louise,

Becky, Alan, Paul and Sanjay... the list is long. They are making an impact, leveraging their advisory/consulting, maximising their profits.

The truth is there is a right way to grow an advisory practice and a wrong way. I make it sound like it could be easy, easy enough maybe to take the ideas in this book and think you know how to run with them.

Now I will be honest with you. Some of you will know how to run with the ideas. Your DNA will be perfect for taking an idea and implementing and getting great results. If this is you then congratulations, please do keep in touch and share your wins with me.

Then there will be some of you who want to implement the new model and the new way to get advisory/consulting clients, and need help to implement.

And this is where we come in.

Here Is How It Works

We do a heap of good for hundreds and hundreds of Practice Owners every year. Right now we have had over 300 people going through our flagship programme Momentum, 100 start-up firms join Get Clients Now and over 250 accountants, bookkeepers and outsourced CFOs use the The Content Lounge 'done-for-you' content marketing.

Our programmes are not right for every practice owner. If you want to offer only compliance services and want to create a Monster Business then we cannot help you. However our ideal client has two things in place:

1. A growth mindset

2. A digital practice that does or wants to deliver advisory/consulting

If this sounds like you, and if you 'get' the fact that you can help people with your expertise in a leveraged way, then you have what it takes to scale your advisory/consulting practice, fast.

Next Steps For You

1. If you are interested in finding out about Momentum and have a turnover of over 5k a month and want to scale your practice send me a message on Linkedin or Facebook with the word Momentum. (details on the next page)

2. If you are a start-up practice with a turnover of less than 5k, right now you need to focus on getting clients. Send me a message on Linkedin or Facebook with the words Get Clients Now.

3. If you are short on time, and want to build your personal and business brand in less than 30 minutes a week join The Content Lounge for 'done-for-you' content marketing. Send me a message on Linkedin or Facebook with the words The Content Lounge.

4. If you would like to join our FREE Facebook group - Superpowers For Accountants, Outsourced CFOs And Financial Coaches then use this link oompf.global/group

5. To watch 100s of video testimonials from successful clients go to oompf.global/success-stories

Whatever your journey looks like moving forward, and whether you choose to work with us or not, I hope that you embrace the concepts and strategies I have shared with you.

Your profession is essential to business owners. They need you now more than ever. They need compliance support, and they need your advice and consulting expertise.

Here is a link to my Facebook personal profile, please connect with me at http://bit.ly/AmandaCWattsFacebook

Here is a link to my Linkedin personal profile, please connect with me at - http://bit.ly/AmandaCWattsLinkedIn

Printed in Great Britain
by Amazon

63863089R00066